CONTENTS

WELCOME TO THE SWEDISH KITCHEN

The Swedish kitchen is not a sanctuary for a chef but rather a family room where people combine cooking with socialising, eating and drinking. Apartments and houses built today often have the kitchen as part of the dining area or living room, and not closed up behind walls. The Swedish kitchen invites families and friends to prepare dinner together, each according to his or her abilities. A child might help out stirring a pot or setting the table, while an older sister or brother might chop vegetables. Even if you are not taking an active part, you are likely to keep the others company, and at least help to sample the food. This book welcomes you into the Swedish kitchen. And don't be surprised if it is occasionally moved outdoors: summer warmth is as precious to Swedes as good food, traditions and new trends.

Swedish food culture is based on great access to local fresh ingredients provided by a countryside that ranges from farmlands to forests and includes a long coastline and a multitude of rivers and lakes. Most of Sweden's open space remains essentially untouched, and the right of public access means that people are free to roam the forests in search for wild berries, herbs and mushrooms.

If you spot a family in the woods with plastic buckets and strange hand-held boxes with a comb-like edge, they are simply out gathering blueberries or lingonberries, using 'berry pickers' to make picking more efficient. Swedes often prefer picking mushrooms in groups, although a favourite secret chanterelle spot is rarely revealed. And after a day in the outdoors, it can be quite nice to sit down and clean the daily catch together. Even top chefs in Sweden frequently gather their own herbs, mushrooms and berries for their restaurants.

The hunting tradition is strong and game such as elk, deer and grouse make popular appearances in the Swedish kitchen. The south and east coasts, rivers and lakes supply a variety of fish such as perch, herring, salmon and trout, while the west coast archipelago is known for its shellfish. Those who have access to water nearby may well also catch their own fish. And to satisfy the demand for local produce, urban farming in cities and towns complement the larger-scale rural farms.

It is no secret that Sweden has a long and dark winter which puts a seasonal dent in local access to most foodstuffs. Despite efficient shipping and global culinary trends that all but eradicate regional food seasons, Swedish cooking still keeps to traditions that include different ways of storing food. Historically a key to survival, food preservation today is used by foodies as an exciting means to culinary delights – preservation methods not only extend shelf life, they also add flavour. It is these particular flavours that attract Swedes to hold on to their methods.

In the spring, summer and autumn Swedes literally harvest more than they can eat. Whereas it used to be a rare delicacy bordering on sinful behaviour to eat fresh berries, Swedes today are more indulgent and able to gormandise in the moment. After all, if all berries from the family foraging in the woods were to be eaten fresh, jams can always be found at the shop.

Fruits and berries are still cooked and preserved, vegetables pickled, mushrooms dried, and meat and fish smoked, salted, fermented and marinated. Long-lasting breads such as dark rye, crisp breads and rusk biscuits have not fallen out of fashion. The same is true of the Swedish fascination with root vegetables such as potatoes and beetroot, once conveniently stored in earth cellars. Fermented milk products are still a popular breakfast food enjoyed with cereals.

The taste for tried and tested foodstuff stops at the ingredients. How they are used is quite a different story. Swedes always hunger for new ideas and inspiration, and often take a traditional ingredient and use it in an unexpected recipe. In this way the Swedish kitchen has managed to transform itself without losing touch with its origins. Indeed, it has lately demanded the attention of the once so predictable culinary Europe, as evidenced by new top class Swedish restaurants (both in Sweden and abroad), by recent successes at international culinary competitions such as the Culinary Olympics and the Bocuse d'Or, and by the attention given by international foodies and magazines.

And at the same time, a lot of restaurants seem to be pizza parlours, Thai kiosks, hamburger places and kebab houses. Not a lot of smoked salmon and cloudberries going on in any of those. Once again, Swedes are curious, always wondering what is cooking on the other side of the globe. Immigrants who bring their own traditions and culinary treats greatly contribute to the range of recipes. It is this meeting of foods, of people, of ideas that truly is the Swedish kitchen.

Let's cook!

FIKA

Swedes prefer not to translate the word *fika*. They don't want it to lose significance and become a mere coffee break. It is one of the first words you will learn when visiting Sweden, right after *tack* (thank you) and *hej* (hello). *Fika* is much more than having a coffee. It is a social phenomenon, a legitimate reason to set aside a moment for quality time. *Fika* can happen at any time, morning as well as evening. It can be savoured at home, at work or in a café. It can be with colleagues, family, friends, or someone you are trying to get to know. It is a tradition observed frequently, preferably several times a day. Accompanying sweets are crucial. Cinnamon buns, cakes, cookies, even open-faced sandwiches pass as acceptable *fika* fare. It comes as no surprise that Swedes are among the top consumers of coffee and sweets in the world – or that Swedes appreciate the good things in life.

Cinnamon bun!

MUM'S APPLE CAKE

Mammas äppelkaka

Apple trees are common in Swedish gardens, orchards and parks. And quite a few of the fruits end up inside apple cakes. It should be enjoyed as it is or with custard.

8–10 PIECES

125 g butter, room temperature
125 g white sugar
2 eggs
150 g plain flour
1 tsp baking powder
1 ml salt
2 tbsp milk
3–4 apples
2 tbsp white sugar plus 2 tbsp ground cinnamon

1. Preheat the oven to 200°C. Grease a round baking pan and coat it with breadcrumbs.

2. Whisk butter and sugar until fluffy, using an electric whisk.

3. Add the eggs one at a time and whisk together with the butter mixture.

4. Fold in flour, baking powder and salt, and stir.

5. Finally, add the milk and stir into a smooth paste. Pour into the pan.

6. Peel, core and slice the apples into sections. Turn them in sugar and cinnamon and place them in the pan with the mixture.

7. Bake for about 30 minutes. Test with a skewer or toothpick to see whether the consistency is right. If it is dry when you pull it out, the cake is ready.

CINNAMON BUNS

Kanelbullar

The cinnamon bun has a day dedicated to it in the Swedish calendar – 4 October. That does not stop Swedes from eating them regularly throughout the year.

45–50 BUNS

150 g butter
500 ml milk, 3%
50 g fresh yeast
1 tsp salt
85 g white sugar
2 tsp crushed cardamom seeds
900 g plain flour

FILLING
100 g butter, room temperature
85 g white sugar
3–4 tbsp ground cinnamon

DECORATION
1 egg, beaten
3–4 tbsp pearl sugar or almond flakes

1. Melt the butter in a saucepan and add the milk. Heat to 37°C.

2. Crumble the yeast in a mixing bowl, pour in the liquid and stir until the yeast dissolves.

3. Add salt, sugar and the crushed cardamom seeds, and almost all the flour. Save a little flour for later.

4. Knead the dough until it is smooth and stretchy and no longer sticks to the edge of the bowl. Let rise under a clean cloth for about 30 minutes.

5. Turn the dough onto a floured surface and cut in two. Roll out into two rectangular shapes about ½ cm thick.

6. Spread on the butter and sprinkle over sugar and cinnamon.

7. From the long side, roll up into two sausages. Cut each roll into chunks so that you get some 45–50 buns altogether, and place them, cut face up, in paper muffin cases on baking sheets. Cover with cloths and leave to rise for a further 30 minutes.

8. Preheat the oven to 225°C. Brush the buns with the egg wash and garnish with pearl sugar or almond flakes.

9. Bake in the middle of the oven for about 8–10 minutes. Leave to cool on wire racks.

CHOCOLATE BALLS

Chokladbollar

Many Swedish youngsters make their kitchen debuts with these childishly delightful chocolate balls.

18–20 BALLS

100 g butter	1 tsp Bourbon pure vanilla powder, or vanilla sugar
2 tbsp cold, strong coffee	
3 tbsp unsweetened cocoa powder	1 ml salt
	DECORATION
120 g rolled oats	200 ml sprinkles, pearl (nib) sugar or shredded coconut
85 g white sugar	

1. Melt the butter.

2. Mix butter and coffee in a large bowl.

3. Add all dry ingredients and mix together. Put the mixture in the fridge for 45 minutes until it is firm enough to roll into balls.

4. Roll 18–20 walnut-sized balls.

5. Pour the decoration of your choice onto a plate and put an empty plate beside it. Roll the balls in the decoration and place them on the empty plate. Cool for 1 hour in the fridge before serving.

CHOCOLATE SHORTBREAD COOKIES

Chokladsnittar

A classic cookie and just one of the seven varieties that Swedish tradition says ought to be served at a coffee party.

50–60 COOKIES

200 g butter, room temperature	1 ml salt
	1 egg yolk
170 g white sugar	300 g plain flour
4 tbsp unsweetened cocoa powder	1 tsp baking powder
	DECORATION
1 tsp Bourbon pure vanilla powder, or vanilla sugar	1 egg, beaten
	100 ml pearl sugar

1. Preheat the oven to 200°C.

2. Stir butter and sugar until fluffy. Add the cocoa, vanilla, salt and egg yolk and mix well.

3. Mix in flour and baking powder and work into a smooth dough.

4. Divide the dough by four and roll into lengths that fit the baking sheet.

5. Place the lengths on the paper-lined baking sheet and flatten them slightly.

6. Brush with beaten egg and sprinkle with pearl sugar. Bake in the middle of the oven for about 10 minutes.

7. Cut the lengths into diagonals while they are still warm.

LENTEN BUNS

Semlor

The Lenten buns known as *semlor* are historically tied to Shrove Tuesday, as the *semla* was the last festive food before Lent. Today even secular Swedes make a religion of eating these delicious buns in the month or so leading up to Easter.

ABOUT 15 LARGE OR 25 SMALL BUNS

100 g butter
300 ml milk, 3%
50 g fresh yeast (for sweet dough)
1 tsp crushed cardamom or the grated peel of 1 orange
½ tsp salt
85 g sugar
about 500–550 g plain flour

1 beaten egg for brushing
FILLING
200 g marzipan
bun centres
100 ml milk
300 ml whipping cream
DECORATION
icing sugar for dusting

1. Melt the butter and add the milk. Heat to 37°C.

2. Crumble the yeast in a bowl and add the cardamom or the orange peel.

3. Add the milky liquid and stir until the yeast has melted. Stir in the salt, the sugar and most of the flour, but save a little flour for later.

4. Work the dough in a food processor/ dough mixer for about 15 minutes.

5. Let it rise to twice its size in the bowl, about 40 minutes.

6. Place the dough on a floured pastry board and cut into pieces. Roll into buns and place on oven paper or greased baking sheet. Let the buns rise to twice their size, about 1 hour.

7. Brush the buns with egg wash. Bake in the lower part of the oven, at 225°C for around 8–10 minutes for large buns and 250°C for 5–7 minutes for small. Leave to cool on wire racks.

8. Cut off the bun tops. Scoop out the centre of each bun (about 2 tsp) and crumble in a bowl.

9. Rough grate the marzipan and mix it with the crumbs and milk into a creamy mass.

10. Fill the hollow buns with this mixture.

11. Whip the cream and squirt or spoon it over the filling. Place the top on the bun and dust with icing sugar.

12. Serve alone with coffee or in the form of a *hetvägg*, that is with warm milk and ground cinnamon.

MIDWEEK DINNER

With both parents working it can be a bit of a family puzzle to pick up the kids, shop for groceries and prepare a wholesome meal, even with a flexible system of parental leave. Many Swedes consider dinner the most robust meal of the day – and it takes place as afternoon turns into evening. As long as everyone in the household helps out, a delicious meal is more than manageable. A Swedish kitchen is often filled with people, not only the designated cook. Very young children may only be silent bystanders with a slice of fruit for appetizer, while the older children take a more active role. Despite the popularity of new and exotic foods there is no denying that classics with roots in the past and the effects of seasons still hold their fort, especially if the kids have their say. Whether an imported fruit or a locally grown root vegetable, many keep their eye out for an organic label.

FISH SOUP WITH SHRIMPS, MUSSELS AND CREAMED HORSERADISH

Fisksoppa med räkor, musslor och pepparrotskräm

Fish soup works well both as an everyday dish and on festive occasions. Serve with a tasty sourdough bread and a mature cheese.

SERVES 4

1 onion	700 g firm fish,
2 cloves of garlic	preferably a mix
1 carrot	of salmon and
1 chilli fruit	white fish
olive oil	500 g precooked
2 tbsp tomato purée	shrimps, unpeeled
100 ml white wine	1 tin, 225 g mussels
300 ml fish stock	salt flakes and
500 g crushed	freshly ground
tomatoes	black pepper
1 tsp dried thyme	1 pinch of sugar

CREAMED HORSERADISH

200 ml crème fraîche
2 tbsp grated horseradish
1 tsp clear honey
1 ml salt

SERVING SUGGESTION:
Sourdough bread and mature cheese

1. Peel and chop the onion, garlic and carrot. Cut open, core and finely chop the chilli.

2. Fry lightly in oil in a large pot but don't brown. Add the tomato purée and let sizzle for another minute or so.

3. Pour in wine, stock, the crushed tomatoes and the thyme, cover and let simmer on low heat for about 10 minutes.

4. Cut the fish into cubes and place in the pot. Cover and simmer for 5 minutes. Peel and add the shrimps and mussels and bring up the heat.

5. Season the soup with salt and pepper and a pinch of sugar. Cream the horseradish and serve on the side.

GAME MEATBALLS WITH SOFT WHEY CHEESE SAUCE

Viltköttbullar med messmörssås

These meatballs melt in your mouth. Meat, sauce and potatoes are suddenly more than just plain fare.

SERVES 4

500 g game mince	1 tsp dried thyme
3 tbsp brown dried breadcrumbs or rolled oats	1 large onion
	2 eggs
150 ml whipping cream	butter for frying
1 tbsp concentrated game stock (fond)	SERVING SUGGESTION:
1 tsp salt	Soft whey cheese sauce, boiled pota-
½ tsp freshly ground juniper berries	toes, raw lingonberry compote and green
1 tsp freshly ground black pepper	vegetables

1. Mix the breadcrumbs or oats with the cream and the stock and leave to rise for 15 minutes. Add the salt and spices.

2. Peel and grate the onion. Fold the mince, onion and eggs into the bread mix and stir carefully.

3. Wet your hands and roll small buns. Place on a rinsed chopping-board. Fry in butter all round for about 4–5 minutes.

SOFT WHEY CHEESE SAUCE

1 small onion	2 tbsp soft whey cheese*, or honey
1 tbsp butter	
800 ml game stock	2–3 tbsp cornflour starch
250 ml whipping cream	salt flakes and freshly ground black pepper
1 tbsp balsamic vinegar	3 tbsp fresh or frozen lingonberries
2 tbsp soya sauce	

1. Peel, chop and lightly brown the onion in butter in a large, broad saucepan.

2. Pour in the stock, whipping cream, balsamic vinegar and soya and let simmer uncovered until reduced by half.

3. Whisk in the whey cheese until it melts and thicken with a little cornflour starch. Season with salt and pepper. Stir in the lingonberries.

* Soft whey cheese (messmör) is a product from northern Sweden made from milk serum, sugar, butter and vanillin. It has a sweet, rounded taste and can be replaced by honey.

Don't forget
the vegetables!

ELK STEW WITH ROOT VEGETABLES AND PRUNES

Älggryta med rotfrukter och katrin-plommon

In autumn, game is a good alternative to beef. There are about 350,000 elk in the wild in Sweden. Their popularity among hunters has to do both with their size, availability and great taste.

SERVES 4–6

1 kg stewing elk cubes	2 tbsp butter
200 g smoked bacon	1 tbsp honey
2 bay leaves	150 g dried prunes
1 tbsp dried thyme	3 tbsp cornflour starch
200 ml red wine	salt and freshly ground black pepper, according to taste, fresh thyme
50 ml balsamic vinegar	
700 ml game stock	
1 onion	SERVING SUGGESTION:
2 medium-sized parsnips	Boiled or creamy mashed potatoes or cooked grain of choice
3 medium-sized carrots	

1. Dice the pork in 1 cm pieces. Heat up a little butter in a large pan and brown the elk and pork cubes together with the bay leaves and thyme, in batches. Transfer it to a large pot and add the wine, balsamic vinegar and game stock. Simmer covered for 1 hour.

2. Peel and cut the onion into quarters and the root vegetables into thick, diagonal slices. Brown them in a little butter. Pour over honey and let sizzle for a few seconds.

3. About 10 minutes before the meat is ready, add the onion, prunes and root vegetables and let everything cook together for the rest of the time. Thicken with the cornflour starch. Season with salt and pepper.

4. Garnish with fresh thyme and serve with boiled or creamy mashed potatoes or cooked grain.

CARBONARA CHANTERELLES   Kantarellcarbonara

A delicious pasta dish in which the smoked bacon has been replaced by crispy chanterelles. It tends to cool rapidly so it should be cooked just before serving. A salad is a welcome addition.

SERVES 4

400 g bavette or tagliatelle	2 handfuls freshly grated, semi-hard cheese, e.g. Väster-botten or parmesan
500 g chanterelles, cleaned and chopped	
butter for frying	1 small bunch chopped leaf parsley
2 cloves of garlic	salt flakes and freshly ground black pepper
200 ml whipping cream	4 egg yolks

1. Cook the pasta according to the instructions on the packet. Drain in a colander but save 100–200 ml of the water in the saucepan.

Put the pasta back in the saucepan with the remaining water and cover to keep warm.

2. Place the mushrooms in a hot, dry pan and fry out the liquid. Add butter, and brown the mushrooms golden at medium heat together with the chopped garlic, about 6–8 minutes.

3. Pour over the cream and cook together for a minute.

4. Fold the mixture in with the pasta, together with the grated cheese. Mix in the parsley. Season with salt and pepper and serve immediately with egg yolks, extra salt flakes and pepper on the side.

GRILL PARTY

Sweden has four distinct seasons, with autumn and winter acting as a pause button for the incredibly popular pastime of outdoor grilling. At the first sign of spring, usually sometime around Walpurgis Night – the traditional spring festival on 30 April – this culinary festivity which lasts into late summer kicks off with a fine glow. With a limited period of sunshine and warm weather, Swedes take every chance they get to be outdoors both cooking and feasting, and their perspective of what can fit on a grill is wide, with everything from fish and vegetables to homemade sausages and cheeses. Stores sell pre-marinated meats and at the checkout counters there are piles of briquettes and single-use miniature grills. Grilling is done in back yards, parks and out in nature. Both a method of adding variation to traditional Swedish cooking and a way to spend time with friends and family, the grill party remains a seasonal treat.

RACK OF LAMB WITH HERB OIL

Lammracks med örtolja

Lamb is perfect for grilling.
If you use a good herb oil, no
marinade is needed.

SERVES 4

1 kg rack of lamb, room temperature
olive oil
salt flakes and freshly ground black pepper
HERB OIL
4 tbsp chopped mint
4 tbsp chopped rosemary
1 organically grown lemon, grated peel
200 ml olive oil
1 tsp clear honey
1 ml salt

1. Get the coals glowing nicely in the grill.

2. Start by mixing together all the herb oil
ingredients. Leave the oil to stand at room
temperature.

3. Divide the rack by cutting between the ribs
and brush the meat surfaces lightly with oil.
Season with salt and pepper.

4. Grill for about 3 minutes on each side.

5. Serve with herb oil and potato salad.

CREAMY COLD SAUCE FOR GRILLED DISHES

Krämig kall sås till grillat

This sauce tastes good with meat,
chicken and fish alike.

SERVES 4–6

100 ml mayonnaise
200 ml crème fraîche
2 tbsp coarse-grained sweet mustard
1 tbsp clear honey
2 tbsp chopped dill
1 tbsp chopped parsley
1 ml salt

Mix everything together and leave to stand
for 1 hour before serving.

Prepare
ahead of time

CREAMY POTATO SALAD

Krämig potatissallad

A great potato salad with plenty of greens goes well with anything off the grill and can be prepared ahead of time in case the grilling happens to take place away from home.

SERVES 4–6

800 g new potatoes
4 spring onions
1 bunch of radish, 125 g
1 bundle of asparagus
150 g mange-tout peas
60 g baby spinach
salt flakes and freshly ground black pepper
DRESSING
200 ml sour cream (*gräddfil*)
3 tbsp mayonnaise
2 tbsp thick, hot and sweet mustard
1 tbsp clear honey
3 tbsp chopped dill
3 tbsp chopped parsley
1 ml salt
DECORATION
fresh crown dill (optional)

1. Wash and boil the potatoes and pour off the water. Let them cool and halve them.

2. Shred the spring onions crossways and cut up the radishes.

3. After breaking off the dry ends of the stalks, parboil the asparagus for about 3–4 minutes in lightly salted water. Rinse under running cold water and cut into pieces.

4. Parboil the mange-touts for a couple of minutes and rinse under cold water.

5. Stir the dressing ingredients together and mix this with the potatoes. Season generously with salt and pepper.

6. Carefully fold in the vegetables, including the baby spinach, but save a little for decoration.

7. Place on an attractive serving dish and top with the remaining vegetables. Garnish with fresh crown dill, if in season.

LEMON-BAKED GRILLED SALMON   Citronbakad lax på grillen

Fish is very popular at a Swedish grill party. With a whole side of salmon, you can cook the entire meal on the grill.

SERVES 6

1 kg salmon fillet, preferably the middle section with skin
3 small organically grown lemons
2 tbsp capers
100 ml olive oil
salt flakes and freshly ground black pepper
PLUS
2 large sheets of grill tin foil

1. Work up a good glow in the grill.

2. Bone the salmon and place it on a double sheet of tin foil with the skin face down.

Season thoroughly with salt and pepper.

3. Wash and thinly slice the lemons. Lay them on the salmon in an overlapping pattern. Strew over the capers and drizzle a little oil on top.

4. Fold up the foil to make a well-sealed package. Place on the grill and bake for about 15–20 minutes, depending on thickness, until the salmon is thoroughly cooked but not dry. Open carefully after 15 minutes and make a small cut in the thickest part to see whether the fish is ready.

5. Serve with potato salad.

BREAKFAST

Most Swedes eat breakfast in their home before heading out to work or school. It is a chance to wake up before setting off into the world. For some that means spending time together with loved ones and for others time for peace and quiet, perhaps a newspaper or social media status. Breakfast flavours are generally mild; bread, coffee and a bowl with yogurt or a dairy product and cereals are often found on a Swedish breakfast table, or perhaps a bowl of oatmeal porridge with fruits or berries. While by many hailed as the most important meal of the day, people's breakfast habits tend to vary greatly, and some might suffice with a cup of coffee and hold on for the ten o'clock *fika* at work. Of all imaginable meals, breakfast is probably the one with least influences from other cultures.

The Swedish kitchen

BREAKFAST

What you might find on a breakfast table in Sweden:

Boiled egg, porridge, muesli, cereals, *filmjölk* (soured milk), yogurt, soft bread, crisp bread, butter, marmalade, hard cheese, cucumber, tomato, *kaviar* (fish roe spread), sliced ham, *leverpastej* (pâté spread), cold cut meats, juice, coffee, tea, milk, smoothie.

CRUNCHY CRISP BREAD WITH CARAWAY

Krispigt knäckebröd med kummin

Sweden has a long tradition in crisp bread baking. The first industrial crisp bread bakery was founded in 1850 but some claim that the bread has been around since 500 AD. The thin, crunchy sheets are suitable for most toppings. For breakfast perhaps simply butter and cheese.

8 SHEETS

50 g fresh yeast	120 g spelt flour
400 ml warm water, 37°C	1 beaten egg for brushing
100 ml rapeseed oil	2 tbsp caraway seeds
1 tsp salt	2 tbsp salt flakes
500 g whole rye flour	

1. Preheat the oven to 200°C.

2. Stir the yeast into the water. Add the oil and salt and stir until the yeast dissolves.

3. Add almost all the flour, a little at a time, and work vigorously into a smooth dough – the food processor may come in handy. Don't let the dough rise.

4. Divide the dough into eight sections and roll out thin sheets the size of dinner plates.

5. Place each section on a baking sheet covered with oven paper and roll out lightly with a deep-notched rolling pin.

6. Brush with egg and sprinkle with caraway seeds and salt.

7. Bake one at a time in the upper part of the oven for about 8–10 minutes. Leave to cool on wire racks. Break into pieces when cool.

FILMJÖLK LOAF WITH LINGONBERRIES

Filmjölkslimpa med lingon

Easy to bake and good for toast the following day. *Filmjölk* is a dairy product made from soured milk. Similar to cultured buttermilk or kefir, it is fermented by different bacteria and has a mild and slightly acidic taste. Cultured buttermilk will work as a substitute.

1 LOAF

40 g rolled oats	natural yogurt or buttermilk
50 g spelt flakes	
120 g wholemeal flour	60 g lingonberries, fresh or frozen
180 g plain flour	65 g hazelnuts, coarsely chopped
1 tsp salt	1–2 tbsp pumpkin seeds for decoration
4 tsp baking powder	
400 ml *filmjölk*,	

1. Preheat the oven to 200°C. Place oven paper in a bread tin that holds about 1½ litres. The paper should fall over the edges of the tin.

2. Mix all the dry ingredients.

3. Add the *filmjölk* and mix together. Fold in the lingonberries and nuts.

4. Pour the mix into the tin and top with pumpkin seeds.

5. Bake for about 50 minutes. Leave to cool on wire racks, under a cloth.

OATMEAL PORRIDGE

Havregrynsgröt

Many Swedes start the day with a bowl of oatmeal porridge. It is especially popular ahead of a day filled with activities. Best served with fresh berries or lingonberry jam.

SERVES 4

150 g rolled oats
900–1,000 ml water
½ tsp salt

SERVING SUGGESTION:
Milk
Lingonberry jam or fresh berries
Raw sugar and/or ground cinnamon (optional)

1. Place all the ingredients in a large saucepan and stir. Bring to the boil and then simmer while stirring for about 3 minutes.

2. Serve with milk, lingonberry jam or fresh berries, and a little raw sugar and cinnamon for that extra taste.

OUTDOOR EATING

Open space and forests make up large parts of Sweden, even around large metropolitan areas. And Swedes love to take advantage of this proximity to nature. Fresh air and exercise are not the only things that bring people outside; *Allemansrätten*, or the right of public access, allows people to forage for food that is not protected or endangered. Of course, there is hunting and fishing, a growing eco-tourism segment for Sweden, but also things you can gather without equipment or special training. Cloudberries (the gold of the marshlands), blueberries, lingonberries, and raspberries are bountiful and easy to find, while mushrooms require more of a trained eye and knowledge. Chanterelles are the most sought-after but the Swedish forests serve up all kinds of delicious fungi. It is also popular to pick herbs and nettles. Even those who do not themselves collect ingredients from the forest will enjoy eating them. And there is no better place for it than outdoors: at a picnic, in a back garden or on a balcony.

MUSHROOM TART

Svamptarte

This mushroom tart is perfect as a starter, a drinks snack or a light lunch with a salad.

SERVES 6–8

1 sheet of ready-made puff pastry, about 30 x 25 cm
300 g mixed mushrooms
butter for frying
2 tsp dried thyme
salt flakes and freshly ground black pepper
1 handful freshly grated Västerbotten
cheese, or other strong, mature cheese
100 ml crème fraîche

DECORATION
crèma di balsamico
wild herbs, e.g. young dandelion leaves, goutweed, cow parsley leaves, yarrow leaves or fresh thyme

1. Preheat the oven to 225°C. Roll out the dough with its paper backing on a baking sheet.

2. Fry the mushrooms in plenty of butter (if newly picked, start by dry-frying without butter so that the liquid is absorbed). Fry the mushrooms at medium heat for about 7–8 minutes. Strew over dried thyme, season generously with salt and pepper.

3. Mix together crème fraîche and grated cheese and spread over the pastry.

4. Add the mushrooms and bake for about 15–20 minutes until the pastry turns golden.

5. Leave to cool for a while, then garnish with crèma di balsamico and wild herbs or fresh thyme. Sprinkle over a few grains of salt and cut the tart into pieces.

mushroom harvest

RASPBERRY AND BLUEBERRY COMPOTE

Drottningkompott

A summer dessert that tastes particularly good after, say, a heavy grill dinner.

SERVES 4

500 g mixed blueberries and raspberries
125 g white sugar
1 tbsp fresh-pressed lemon juice
1 vanilla pod, seeds and pod

SERVING SUGGESTION:
Half-and-half cream or vanilla ice cream

1. Put the berries in a saucepan with sugar and lemon juice.

2. Scrape out the seeds of vanilla pod. Add both seeds and pod to the sauce pan.

3. Simmer gently, uncovered, for about 30 minutes until the compote thickens. Stir occasionally.

4. Serve with half-and-half cream or vanilla ice cream.

NETTLE SOUP Nässelsoppa

The wonder of nature in a soup. Who would have thought that weeds could taste so good.

SERVES 4

2 litres or 100 g fresh, cleaned nettles
1 onion
2 tbsp olive oil
700 ml strong chicken or vegetable stock
100 ml whipping cream
1–2 tbsp potato starch plus a little cold water
salt flakes and freshly ground black pepper

SERVING SUGGESTION:
8 quail eggs

1. Chop up the nettles and the onion. Fry them in the oil in a large saucepan for about 4–5 minutes.

2. Pour in the stock and cream and leave to combine for 5 minutes.

3. Dissolve the starch in a little cold water and whisk it into the soup. Bring the soup rapidly to the boil until it thickens slightly. Season with salt and pepper.

4. Boil the quail eggs for one minute. Rinse in ice-cold water, peel and cut in two. Serve the halves in the soup.

MEADOWSWEET CORDIAL

Älggrässaft

A beautiful weed yields a magically tasty cordial with a slight tang of bitter almonds and lemon.

3 LITRES OF FRUIT SYRUP

50 clusters of meadowsweet flowers
2 kg white sugar
2 litres water
60 g citric acid
2 organically grown lemons

1. Rinse the flowers in cold water and put them in a jar large enough to hold about five litres.

2. Boil sugar and water until the sugar dissolves, and leave to cool. Mix in the citric acid.

3. Brush the lemons under running hot water, slice and put in the jar with the flower clusters. Pour in the sugar liquid.

4. Put on the lid, or a plate, and place the jar in a cool place for 6–7 days. Stir every day.

5. Strain into clean bottles. Stored in the fridge, the syrup lasts for several months.

CRISPY FRIED PERCH ON CRISP BREAD

Knaperstekt abborre på knäckebröd

Should you happen to catch a perch, all you need is a buttered slice of crisp bread to go with it.

SERVES 4

4 large perch fillets
2 eggs
100 g brown dried breadcrumbs (*ströbröd*)
1 tsp salt, freshly ground white pepper
butter for frying

1. Beat the eggs. Mix the breadcrumbs with salt and a little pepper and place on a dish.

2. Turn the fillets in the eggs and then in the breadcrumb mixture.

3. Brown the fillets in plenty of butter on both sides and serve with buttered crisp bread. Eat straight away.

SERVING SUGGESTION:
Crisp bread and butter

LUNCH

Whether at work or in school, or at home at the weekend, a Swedish lunch typically means a proper cooked meal. That also means setting aside enough time to be able to enjoy it. Swedish law ensures that elementary schools provide nutritional lunches free of charge to all pupils. Most preschools and secondary schools follow the same guidelines. It is quite common to allow students to serve themselves the portion they want, and to provide a vegetarian alternative. Adults in the workplace rarely have the luxury of a lunch provided free of charge by an employer, and instead have to choose whether to spend part of a Sunday cooking up boxed meals for the working week, to bring daily leftovers – or head out to a restaurant. Most restaurants have lunch specials at a favourable price. Whether lunch is taken at the workplace or a restaurant, coffee is usually available for free. While the weekend brunch is gaining momentum in Swedish restaurants, the era of a home-cooked weekend lunch is far from over.

ROOT VEGETABLE HASH BROWNS WITH BACON AND LINGONBERRIES

Rotfruktsraggmunkar med bacon och lingon

Raggmunkar, or crisp hash browns, with salty bacon and sourish lingonberries is a classic Swedish lunch.

SERVES 4

120 g plain flour	400 g carrots
400 ml milk	butter for frying
1 tsp salt	SERVING SUGGESTION:
1 egg	Fried bacon
400 g potatoes	Lingonberry jam

1. Whisk the flour and salt into half of the milk.

2. Whisk in the rest of the milk to make a lump-free mixture. Whisk in the egg.

3. Peel and coarse-grate the potatoes and carrots. Squeeze out any surplus liquid through a strainer.

4. Add the grated potatoes and carrots to the batter and mix well. Fry hash browns in butter at medium heat until they are golden, a couple of minutes on each side. Serve with bacon and lingonberries.

Tip!

If you want to make your own lingonberry jam, just boil 1 kilo of cleaned lingonberries in 200 ml of water for about 8–10 minutes. Remove the scum and add 500 grams of white sugar. Stir until the sugar dissolves. Ladle the jam into clean, warm glass jars and put on the lid. If kept cool in the fridge, the jam will last for several months.

YELLOW PEA SOUP

Ärtsoppa

Yellow pea soup is an excellent vegetarian alternative, but it can also be served in the traditional Swedish way with lightly salted ham hocks or pork sausage in it. Thursday is the traditional day for pea soup, with pancakes, and sometimes even punch liqueur, for dessert. This large batch is perfect for freezing, in case you want to bring some to work.

SERVES 10

500 g dried yellow peas	2 onions
2 litres water	2 large carrots
2 vegetable stock cubes	3 tbsp fresh, chopped thyme plus a little extra for decoration

1. Soak the peas in cold water for about 10–12 hours.

2. Pour off the water and rinse the peas in a strainer. Put them in a large saucepan, add 2 litres of water and bring to the boil.

3. Crumble in the stock cubes, cover and leave to simmer at medium heat for 30 minutes.

4. Meanwhile, peel and quarter the onions and peel and slice the carrots. Add them with the thyme and allow to boil for another 30 minutes. Taste to see whether a little salt is required and whether the peas are soft.

5. Serve with a quality mustard and perhaps a little more thyme.

OVEN PANCAKE

Ugnspannkaka

Much thicker and with a unique taste, an oven pancake is easier to make than a frying pan version. It is perfect after the pea soup. It is also popular to eat oven pancake with bacon and lingonberry jam.

SERVES 6

150 g plain flour
½ tsp salt
600 ml milk
3 eggs

1. Preheat the oven to 225°C. Grease an ovenproof dish of about 30 x 22 cm.

2. Put the flour and salt in a bowl and whisk in half the milk to make a lump-free paste. Add the rest of the milk while continuing to whisk. Lastly, add the eggs and stir to a smooth blend.

3. Pour the mixture into the dish and bake in the middle of the oven for about 25 minutes until the pancake is golden and puffs up.

4. Cut into pieces and serve with jam or apple sauce and a carrot salad on the side.

JUICY CARROT SALAD

Saftig morotssallad

Really tasty with the pancake. And nutritious, too.

SERVES 6

2–3 large carrots
1 orange
50 ml raisins

1. Peel and coarse-grate the carrots.

2. Halve the orange and squeeze out the juice of one half. Cut the other half into 6 pieces.

3. Mix the carrot with the orange juice and raisins. Serve with the pancake, with a piece of orange alongside.

COSY FRIDAY

In the 1990s, the term *fredagsmys*, or cosy Friday, established itself in the Swedish consciousness. The expression stems from a long tradition of making the start of the weekend a bit special in combination with… a marketing campaign for crisps. Terminology aside, it is a much-needed way to mark the end of the working week and gear up for the weekend. It is a culinary semicolon. *Fredagsmys* takes on different shapes depending on who it is for: a couple, a family with kids, and friends will all have their own variation. A key ingredient, however, is easy meals for which everyone is the master chef. Finger food and snacks are preferred to cooking and cleaning a pile of dirty pots and pans. On a Wednesday evening the kids may sit in front of the computer while the parents are busying themselves in the kitchen, but on Friday it is all about time together. Many also associate *fredagsmys* with watching television.

QUESADILLAS WITH SMOKED ROAST REINDEER

Quesadillas med rökt renstek

A perfect snack that once again exemplifies the successful mixture of local flavours with new trends. Mexican food is a popular starting point in Swedish kitchens, with less chilli and more reindeer. Game meat can work as an alternative if reindeer is a challenge to find.

16 PIECES

4 large flour tortillas
2 handfuls freshly grated Swedish Västerbotten cheese*
200 g smoked roast reindeer, thinly sliced
30 g rocket
butter for frying

1. Lay out two of the tortillas and sprinkle the cheese on top.

2. Add the roast reindeer and the rocket. Place the other two tortillas on top and press lightly together.

3. Heat up butter in a large pan and fry each double tortilla for about a minute on both sides. If you like, press lightly with a spatula so that the contents melt together.

4. Place on a chopping-board and cut each into eight pieces.

* Västerbotten cheese takes its name from the province of Västerbotten, West Bothnia, in the north of Sweden. It is a hard cow's milk cheese with a firm texture and a high fat content. The long maturation period on spruce shelves gives it its distinct character and strong flavour.

tip!
You can add cold-smoked or dry-cured ham as extra topping after the pizza is prepared.

PIZZA WITH MUSHROOMS AND SPINACH

Pizza med svamp och spenat

In Sweden, pizza parlours are found in every town, every neighbourhood, and they have incredibly imaginative toppings (such as kebab meat with French fries or filet mignon with Béarnaise sauce). But Swedes also love home-made pizzas, which open up for personal exploration in terms of toppings. It is a perfect meal to make together with family or friends. Try to make the base as thin as possible, the Swedish way.

1 BATCH/4 PORTION PIZZAS

25 g fresh yeast
250 ml water, 37°C
1 tsp sea salt
1 tbsp olive oil
350 g strong white bread flour
500 g fresh mushrooms

2 tbsp butter for frying
5 handfuls freshly grated cheese, mature, semi-hard
60 g baby spinach
olive oil
salt flakes and freshly ground black pepper

1. Dissolve the yeast in the warm water. Add the sea salt and olive oil and blend in a food processor until the yeast has been completely absorbed.

2. Add the flour a little at a time and work the dough vigorously until it no longer sticks to the edge of the bowl and is smooth and shiny, about 10 minutes. Leave to rise under a cloth for 30 minutes until it has doubled in size.

3. Meanwhile, cut up and fry the mushrooms at medium heat for about 7–8 minutes. If you are using mushrooms that you have picked yourself, you should begin by 'dry-frying' all the liquid out before adding the butter. Season generously with salt and pepper.

4. Lightly knead the dough and divide into four. Roll and press it out and try to get it as thin as possible.

5. Preheat your oven to 250°C.

6. Spread the cheese and mushrooms on the base. Top with spinach and bake the pizzas for about 10 minutes until they begin to brown at the edges. Drizzle a little olive oil on top and serve.

WRAPS WITH RAW SPICED SALMON (*GRAVLAX*) AND YOGURT-DILL SAUCE

Wraps med gravad lax och dillyoghurt

So simple – a whole meal in a bread wrap. A very good example of how Swedes love to mix tradition (*gravlax*) with new influences (wrap). Try cold-smoked salmon if you don't like *gravlax*.

4 WRAPS

4 large rounds of flat bread, freshly baked
200 g *gravlax*, thinly sliced, or cold-smoked salmon
70 g mixed pieces of lettuce
freshly ground black pepper

YOGURT-DILL SAUCE
1 apple, cored and peeled
3 tbsp chopped dill
200 ml strained yogurt, 10%
1 tsp clear honey

1. Start by finely chopping the apple and mixing it with all the sauce ingredients into a dill cream.

2. Lay out the bread and spread the pieces of lettuce, salmon and dill cream on top. Add a light sprinkling of pepper.

3. Fold up one of the edges of the bread and wrap round so that the sides overlap.

4. Wrap a little tin foil round the base to keep everything together.

Making your own *gravlax* is easy if you prepare it in advance. You need 1 kilo of fresh, boned salmon fillet with the skin intact. Mix 4 tablespoons of salt with 4 tablespoons of white sugar and 2 teaspoons of freshly ground white pepper. Rub the mixture into the salmon and strew 3 tablespoons of finely chopped fresh or frozen dill over the flesh side. Wrap the salmon in double layers of cling film and place in a dish. Leave to marinate in the fridge for 48 hours. Turn occasionally. Scrape off any excess seasoning and slice the salmon into thin, diagonal pieces.

RHUBARB PIE WITH STRAWBERRIES

Rabarberpaj med jordgubbar

Strawberries and rhubarb are a fantastic combination. The tartness of the rhubarb is balanced by the sweetness of the strawberries...and some added sugar.

1 LARGE PIE, ABOUT 6 PORTIONS, OR 6 PORTION TINS

CRUMBLE
40 g rolled oats
60 g plain flour
100 g cold unsalted butter, diced
1 ml salt

FILLING
200 g rhubarb
200 g strawberries
85 g white sugar

1 tsp organic Bourbon vanilla powder
1 tsp ground cinnamon
3 tbsp potato starch

SERVING SUGGESTION:
Fine, high-quality vanilla ice cream or whipped cream

1. Preheat the oven to 225°C. Pinch the ingredients into a coarse crumble.

2. Cross-cut the rhubarb stalks into slices of about 1 cm and place in a large bowl. Halve the strawberries and place them in the bowl, too. Add the sugar and mix in the vanilla powder, cinnamon and starch.

3. Grease a large baking tin or portion tins and add the rhubarb mix. Spread the crumble on top and bake for about 15–20 minutes until the dough is crisp.

4. Serve with vanilla ice cream or cream.

DINNER PARTY

A Swedish dinner party is often a casual and relaxed event, a chance for friends to socialise and share a few laughs. But you can be certain that the host will sharpen his or her culinary skills and concoct something with a little extra flair for both taste buds and eyes to feast on. It is a chance to break free from the limitations of a hectic working week and focus entirely on food and pleasure. Keen observers of a Swedish dinner party will notice a few formalities. Shoes, for example, are normally left at the door. Someone might bring indoor shoes for the occasion. Toasts follow a careful ritual, with each person making eye contact with everyone else before drinking. Clothing varies according to personal choice, and it is not unusual to see denim next to a suit and tie. That Swedes need a little time to warm up is evident in the more liberal distribution of hugs at the end of the party compared to the beginning. The following recipes work splendidly to set you up for a truly Swedish dinner party.

KAVRING CROSTINIS WITH GOAT'S CHEESE AND CLOUDBERRIES

Kavring crostini med getost och hjortron

Kavring is a dark rye bread from southern Sweden that is sweetened with syrup. Its crispy surface and the salty cheese are a perfect combination. The cloudberries offer a tart contrast.

12 CROSTINIS

12 slices dark rye bread (*kavring*)
1 tbsp butter
200 g Swedish goat's cheese
100 ml cloudberry jam or raw cloudberry compote
12 small sprigs of leaf parsley

1. Cut out rounds of bread, using a dram glass, for instance.

2. Heat up the butter and fry the rounds rapidly on both sides so that they become crisp.

3. Cut the cheese into 12 slices and place on the bread.

4. Top with cloudberries and garnish with parsley.

Tip!

If you want to make raw cloudberry compote yourself, just mix 100 grams of fresh or frozen berries with 100 ml of white sugar and let it stand in the fridge for a couple of hours. Stir occasionally.

Starter

AVOCADO AND ROCKET SALAD WITH WHITEFISH ROE

Avokado- och ruccolasallad med löjrom

Kalix Löjrom, a whitefish roe, or vendace caviar, specifically harvested from the archipelago of the Gulf of Bothnia in northern Sweden, is one of two Swedish products with a status of Protected Designation of Origin issued by the European Union. Whitefish roe is also found in many inland lakes throughout Sweden, as well as in certain parts of Europe. A small appetiser featuring salty whitefish roe and mild avocado makes a good start to the meal.

SERVES 4

80 g whitefish roe
1 large ripe avocado pear
1 small red onion
50 g rocket
1 tbsp olive oil
4 tbsp soured cream (*gräddfil*) or crème fraîche
salt flakes and freshly ground black pepper
DECORATION
4 sprigs of dill
4 wedges of lemon

1. Halve the avocado, remove the pip, and peel.

2. Cut into slices.

3. Peel and finely chop the onion.

4. Mix the rocket with the olive oil.

5. Place alternate layers of rocket and avocado in the centre of four plates and top with whitefish roe and a dollop of soured cream or crème fraîche. Sprinkle with the finely chopped onion.

6. Garnish with dill sprigs and a wedge of lemon. Season lightly with salt and pepper.

7. If desired, serve with a thin slice of toast.

Main course

OVEN-BAKED COD WITH BROWN BUTTER, SHRIMPS AND GRATED HORSERADISH

Rimmad ugnsbakad torsk med brynt smör, räkor och riven pepparrot

Fresh cod, shrimps and horseradish. Swedish luxury.

SERVES 4

800 g cod loin in portion pieces, with skin
600 g precooked shrimps, unpeeled
BRINE
5 tbsp salt
1 litre water
BROWN BUTTER
200 g butter
SERVING SUGGESTION:
Boiled new potatoes
Grated horseradish
Lightly boiled mange-tout peas
DECORATION
4 sprigs of dill
4 wedges of lemon
4 precooked shrimps, unpeeled

1. Mix the salt and water and stir until the salt has dissolved.

2. Add the pieces of fish and place in the fridge for 1 hour.

3. Peel the shrimps but save four for the decoration.

4. Preheat the oven to 125°C.

5. Take the fish out of the brine and place it in a greased ovenproof dish with the skin facing down. Leave the fish in the oven until its inner temperature is 56°C, or about 15 minutes.

6. Brown the butter in a saucepan until it is golden and smells of nut. Skim off the scum with a spoon.

7. Serve immediately with shrimps, brown butter and freshly grated horseradish. Serve with potatoes and lightly boiled mange-touts. Garnish each plate with a whole shrimp, sprigs of dill and wedges of lemon.

Dessert

SALTED TOFFEE PIE WITH FROZEN BLACKBERRIES

Saltad kolapaj med frysta björnbär

Swedes love to mix sweet and salt. Here is a sweet finish with a salt twist. If you like, you can serve a dollop of crème fraîche with it. Remember to prepare this dessert well in advance. It is certainly worth the wait.

8–10 SLICES

125 g butter
2 tbsp icing sugar
180 g plain flour
1 egg yolk
1 tbsp cold water
FILLING
300 ml whipping cream
135 g cane sugar
210 g syrup, dark or light
75 g butter, diced
DECORATION
1 tsp salt flakes
70 g frozen blackberries

1. Chop the butter, icing sugar and flour together, or blend with a food processor.

2. Add the egg yolk and water. Work swiftly into a dough. Press into a pie tin, preferably one with a detachable rim.

3. Preheat the oven to 225°C. Bake the pie crust for about 12 minutes until it gains a little colour.

4. Pour the cream, cane sugar and syrup into a thick-bottomed saucepan and let simmer at medium heat for about 30–40 minutes until the mix thickens slightly.

5. Check whether the toffee is ready by releasing a couple of drops of the mixture into a glass of water. If the toffee congeals and you can make a little ball out of it, it is ready. Otherwise, simmer for a little longer. Stir in the butter until it melts. Let the toffee sauce cool at room temperature for half an hour.

6. Pour the toffee mix into the pie tin, sprinkle over the salt and let the pie set in the fridge for 1 hour. The mass should be firm but not hard.

7. Take it out for a while before serving and garnish with frozen blackberries.

LISELOTTE FORSLIN is a freelance food writer, food stylist and author of several cookbooks. She is passionate about food and communication and creates recipes that most people should feel comfortable with. Liselotte's food is easy to prepare, reasonably healthy and of course delicious.

RIKARD LAGERBERG is a Swedish writer with roots in San Francisco, Stockholm and Sligo, who, after years of a typical Swedish diet, chose a vegetarian direction for himself in the 90s. He currently prepares to get his hunting license, not sure himself whether that will mean a shift in diet. Will he pull the trigger once face to face with the king of the forest?

SUSANNE WALSTRÖM is a photographer based in Sweden, but with agents in both New York and Stockholm, she travels to wherever the next shoot may be. Her background in documentary work and news journalism helps her capture natural interactions in a colourful and simple way. Her personal documentary style has been applied to a multitude of subjects, including several books about food.

ABOUT THE SWEDISH INSTITUTE

The Swedish Institute (SI) is a public agency that promotes interest and confidence in Sweden around the world. SI seeks to establish cooperation and lasting relations with other countries through strategic communication and exchange in the fields of culture, education, science and business. SI works closely with Swedish embassies and consulates around the world. For more information about SI and Sweden, please visit Si.se and Sweden.se.

Sharingsweden.se offers a comprehensive collection of materials about Sweden, produced by the Swedish Institute.

Do you have any views on this SI publication? Feel free to contact us at order@si.se.